STRINGS ATTACHED

Made in Michigan Writers Series

STRINGS ATTACHED

POEMS BY

Diane DeCillis

WAYNE STATE UNIVERSITY PRESS

DETROIT

18 17 16 15 14   5 4 3 2 1

ISBN 978-0-8143-4013-4 (paperback) / ISBN 978-0-8143-4014-1 (e-book)

Library of Congress Control Number: 2013950621

∞

Publication of this book was made possible by
a generous gift from *The Meijer Foundation*.

Designed by *Andrew Kopietz*
Typeset by *Charlie Sharp, Sharp Des!gns, Lansing, MI*
Composed in *FF Scala* and *DIN Next LT Pro* typefaces

For Louie, Mom and Dad

Contents

Acknowledgments   xi

I

Margin of Error   3

The Myth of Father   4

As Pressing Is to Flowers   6

In a Dream My Skin   8

Still Life Flowering   9

The Way You Look   10

Seeing Like Cézanne   12

View from a Room, NYC   13

Fugitive Laughter   14

Quiet Rooms   15

Agoraphobia Contrapuntal   16

Finding Fathers   17

Postcards of Home and Homesick   19

Childhood Revisited as a Musical   21

Dreams of My Father   22

Lost on the Champs-Élysées   23

La Vie en Gris   24

Reconsidering Yellow   25

When You Cannot Sleep   27

Foreboding Frog   29

Physics for Dummies   30

Mr. Right   32

Falling in Love at the Speed of the William Tell "Overture"   33

An Orgasm Is a Terrible Thing to Waste   34

Punch Drunk Love   36

Touching the Wound   37

Last Night I Dreamed I Stole the Croissants   38

Power of Suggestion   40

Happy-Go-Lucky   41

To Lean   42

Thinking about What Matters   43

II

Milk   47

Without Child   49

Room Full of Children Staring at Me   50

The Grammar of Memory   52

Arranged Marriage   53

Yellow According to Rilke   55

Artemesia Absinthium   56

Weeping Women   57

Cubist Still Life   59

Origami Pantoum   60

Looking for Stephen Dunn   61

Body Language 62

Lee Miller's Father 64

Phantom Limbs 65

Nest 67

Creation of Birds 69

Magritte's Mother's Nightgown 70

A Day at the Lake with Gertrude Stein 71

Defitato 72

Fish Feel Pain 74

When Chefs Have Nightmares 76

Ingratiating the Monster 78

What Would Hitchcock Do? 79

Missing Ingredients 81

Grape Leaves 83

The Meaning of Life 85

How to Fall Gently from the Precarious Pedestal 86

The Botanist and Her Amaryllis 88

To Be Fed 89

Baklava Killed My Father 90

Music from Another Room 93

Strings Attached 94

ACKNOWLEDGMENTS

I am grateful to the editors of the following journals for first publishing these poems, some in slightly different versions.

A Gathering of Tribes: "Nest"; *Ascent*: "Touching the Wound"; *Bayou*: "When You Cannot Sleep"; *Borderlands: Texas Poetry Review*: "To Be Fed"; *Cadillac Cicatrix*: "Defitato"; *CALYX*: "Quiet Rooms"; *Cape Rock*: "The Grammar of Memory"; *Connecticut Review*: "Magritte's Mother's Nightgown"; *Drumvoices Revue*: "Grape Leaves"; *Eclipse*: "Origami Pantoum"; *Evansville Review*: "La Vie en Gris"; *Flint Hills Review*: "Falling in Love at the Speed of the *William Tell* 'Overture'"; *Gargoyle*: "A Day at the Lake With Gertrude Stein"; *Gastronomica*: "Missing Ingredients"; *Green Hills Literary Lantern*: "Fish Feel Pain"; *George Washington Review*: "Margin of Error"; *The MacGuffin*: "Arranged Marriage," "Cubist Still Life," "Postcards of Home and Homesick," "An Orgasm Is a Terrible Thing to Waste," "What Would Hitchcock Do?," "Seeing Like Cézanne," and "Yellow According to Rilke"; *Madison Review*: "Milk"; *Nimrod*: "Childhood Revisited as a Musical" and "Looking for Stephen Dunn"; *North Atlantic Review*: "In a Dream My Skin"; *Owen Wister Review*: "How To Fall Gently from the Precarious Pedestal"; *Pisgah Review*: "Mr. Right"; *Poet Lore*: "Dreams of My Father"; *Sanskrit*: "Music from Another Room"; *Schuylkill Valley Journal*: "The Meaning of Life" and "Last Night I Dreamed I Stole the Croissants"; *Scriblerus Press*: "Physics for Dummies"; *Slipstream*: "Punch Drunk Love"; *Soundings East*: "Reconsidering Yellow"; *South Carolina Review*: "Weeping Women"; *South Dakota Review*: "Lee Miller's Father"; *Spillway*: "Lost on the Champs-Élysées"; *Sulphur River Literary Review*: "Creation of Birds" and "Without Child"; *Westview*: "Happy-Go-Lucky"; *Yalobusha Review*: "The Way You Look"; *Zone 3*: "To Lean"

A heartfelt thank-you to the following friends and peers who were generously supportive in the making of these poems: Mary Jo Firth Gillett, Elizabeth Volpe, Rebecca Rank Perry, Christine Rhein, Carol Was, Sharron Singleton, Mindy La Pere, and the talented poets in the Tuesday night group. A special thank-you to Annie Martin and the staff at WSU Press for their kind support, to Rafal Olbinski for his marvelous artwork, to John D.Lamb for nurturing us with Springfed Arts, and to M. L. Liebler for making Detroit an enviable literary and music force.

How do we not go crazy,
we who have found ourselves compelled
to live with the circle, the ellipsis, the word
not yet written.

STEPHEN DUNN

Margin of Error

is the land I live in. Landscape of uncertainty
I can tolerate. It's right brain, not left,
Left Bank, not West Bank. Land of doubt
not dogma. It's The Flying Wallendas
with a net. Those who fall in love
again. Place where slim to nil was once
fat chance. Give me elbowroom, latitude
and leeway—the bungee, not the noose.
Pollock's drips, not Vermeer's precision—
Ella's scat, and Sagan's stars. Perhaps,
perchance—the stuff of pinches, dashes,
smidges—written in sand not stone.
The crossword done in pencil, the white
on the page—the forecaster who gets it
wrong—the horoscope that gets it right.
It isn't knowledge of the speed of light, but
intuition of the weight of darkness. Three
out of five, and Saturn V—the guy who asks,
What are the chances you'd marry me?
And to the reply of one in a million says,
Okay. So there's hope.

The Myth of Father

If my father only knew
how I am
just like him
how I soak up
the air
like air,
how the moon
excites me
like the distant lands
that pulled him away.

What is there to love
about craters I asked
before I fell
in love with craters,
before he traveled
across oceans,
and I discovered
the extravagance
of oceans.

When I speak
in the realm of father,
I speak from
the vantage point
of craters. Like him
I am adept
at sleight of being,
an alien familiar
with dodging
horizons, familiar
with the carbonic
taste of loss

and the crater smell
which can only be

described as lacking
any hint of core
or surface.

Yet looking up
at the moon
I remember
my father's scent,
and I want to ask him
something ordinary,
like, what did you
have for lunch
the day you left?
I had air, which
you might have
mistaken for air.
It was just me,
my long whisper,
none of this is real.

As Pressing Is to Flowers

The only precious thing I own, this pressed flower
tray from Lebanon, where trays like this are made
by people with names like Hajaili, my Lebanese name
which I recently discovered translates to Partridge.
So I'm from the Partridge family, but my last name,
Shipley, after my grandfather's middle name. It's
no wonder I'm a girl with no sense of direction, map
challenged, who cherishes the inheritance of a tray from
a father who wanted me to come to Lebanon to marry
my intended . . . well, his intended—a good Druze man.

Under my breath I'd sing a good "Druze" man is hard
to find —especially since I lived in Detroit, and was
baptized Unitarian. We served meals on this tray—
snacks and drinks the Lebanese artisan wasn't
picturing when she pressed oval glass over a micro
meadow of wheat stalks and wildflowers gathered
from the Bekáa valley. Flowers that inherited yellows,
pinks, and violets—somehow remembering their genomes
even as they fade. Often we poured Maxwell House,

not rich Turkish coffee, cardamom flavored and with
a cup-reading at the end—a bonus like the prize
in Cracker Jack, back when they gave ornate bird whistles
and decoder rings, not the disappointing paper thingies
you get today. Usually, Lipton, not *meghle*, tea brewed
with cinnamon sticks, ginger, anise, and orange rind studded
with cloves—its exotic bouquet wafting from the kitchen
like a belly dancer's scarves. I say Maxwell House coffee
is to Turkish coffee as Twinkies are to baklava, crisp Lebanese
baklava made with chopped pistachios, drizzled with fragrant

rosewater syrup. I must admit I've always loved those
little sponge cakes—felt bad when the company went
bankrupt. Twinkies are to America as stability is to Lebanon,
though arguably since they're preserved to last forever. But

this tray, the one thing I took when I left home, is my only
palpable connection to my father, a man my New York
mother married in Beirut, a good Druze man who shouldn't
have been intended for her. I say rubble is to buildings
as marriage is to parents, as pressing is to flowers,
as flowers are to fading, as fading is to what remains.

In a Dream My Skin

seemed like rag paper, the kind
that absorbs watercolors.
Every so often a vein would
hemorrhage beneath the flesh
of my forearm. I'd watch it
spread the way ink spreads
on a blotter, as if my pulse,
my heart was made visible.
I couldn't stop the bleeding,
and the doctors didn't know
what to do. Hard to resist
watching it, a scarlet peony
blooming fast-forward
as if death had considered
my love of beauty.

Still Life Flowering

It was the moment my boss
thumped a large watermelon
onto the white Formica counter,

as if green had arrived—its skin,
a dark forest with Monet dabs
of light hinting at what's inside.

I saw the knife plunge into the center.
Unable to penetrate the whole of it,
he used his surgeon hands to

crack the rest apart, the sound
of it like the earth splitting. And then
it all went very different for a girl

taught to respect boundaries,
the way this fruit was contained
within its thick rind. He didn't

slice it—he gouged the heart
out, eating it with a hunger
I had never seen—the juice

shored between his lips. Carving
the next bite, it seemed
to flower from his fingertips.

I stood there, white uniform,
white nurse's shoes, eyeing
him and the red blossom

he laid into my mouth,
the sweet fruit and all
those slippery black seeds.

The Way You Look

I was the young girl who dropped acid with her boss,
    a doctor who said he was experimenting for research.
He noticed I looked Japanese under the influence,
    which was interesting because my Lebanese

mother looked Asian in certain pictures.
    The doctor and I became a couple, stayed together
for years. He was older than my father,
    a foot taller than me, and Irish. His skin, fair

next to my olive complexion, shoe size
    nearly twice my size 7's. But studying
our photos we saw a strong resemblance—
    our smile, the eyes, and he noticed we both

had freckles, a sort of connect-the-dots that formed
    a bond. I wondered if this likeness had always
been there or if it grew out of the desire to merge.
    I've never been photogenic. Hard for me

to pose. I try wide eyes, broad smile, chin up,
    chin down, it's just not good. They say symmetry
is key, "the golden ratio," of beauty,
    high cheek bones, nice teeth—traits

models and actors possess. "Echoism"
    is an influence in attraction. Those
who share similar features are drawn
    to an echo of their own face. It happens

with dogs and their owners. And Prima Copulism:
    the allure that attracts us to someone
whose face reminds us of first love—
    father or mother. I've never told anyone

about our acid trips. It opens your mind to a wild
    mosaic. Once, driving to the store, Doc saw
a dead animal in the road. I asked if it was an elephant
    and he said it was. We both saw the dead giraffe,

the zebras, and lions. On acid you can say
    the word geisha and watch origami unfold a girl
in a red kimono patterned in live birds. The Japanese
    say it's impolite to show affection openly,

better to express it with restraint. But I say
    love has no manners or measure—
it's the heart that chews with its mouth open,
    the animal that drinks with its eyes.

Seeing Like Cézanne

There's this thing you've always wanted
to write about— the circle, the square,
the triangle. You think you see the way
Cézanne's mind worked, a pair of shears

cutting countrysides into shapes—
the river a rectangle, mountain a cone.
He never meant for the apple to make
you hungry.
                    Mondrian learned from him—
flattening city streets, blocks of saturated
color, taxi-yellow dots, tar-black lines,
buildings rubbled to their essence.

You see a dim square of light,
an office late at night, someone
working on a deadline, or not
wanting to go home.
                    You see a mother's
hand sweep a brow, the line of a small
mouth curving. And dawn, the color
of old medicine—tincture of iodine.

You see a fever and a hunger
that never leaves. You see sky, captive
sky gathering words that burn and rise,

smoke-gray clouds,
                    red circle sun—

the fire in your belly. It means something.

View from a Room, NYC

I've long liked the image of a fleabag motel and once
stayed at one with the boy I was sure I'd marry. It had
a spare charm with its thin walls and total lack
of amenities. No Starbucks on a counter that doubles as
a desk, no fitness room, no Vivaldi in the lobby. No lobby.

There's something seductive about those old neon signs
glowing like beacons in the dark—a setting where secrets
are written with stars on a chalkboard sky. Movie motels
where the Sandra Dee/Tab Hunter couple who've been
aching to play footsy insist they need two rooms (car
broke down). But jeepers—there's only one room left.

The jaded clerk with a cigarette dangling from his pout
barely looks up, says, "Yeah, yeah, sign here." So Tab
sleeps on the floor while Sandy squirms in the bed above
like some angel about to take a fall.
                              Cut to the Don Draper
type: sexy voice, slick hair, custom suits. He walks in
like a Do Not Disturb sign, scribbling the register with an alias
so none—mainly Mrs. D— will suspect he's bedding up
with Chanel Le Bop, the floozy with a PhD in understanding.
But my room tonight has none of that. There's a window

with a view of wet, lacquered streets rubified by signs that say
Luigi's Pizza, Tony's Pizza, Joey's Pizza, all owned by somebody
who's not Italian. And I'm feeling like Moll, not the sexy mistress
of some gangster on the lam, just a girl in a tank top lookin'
for some shuteye in this room, where my companion is insomnia—
and the wake-up call, sunrise wedging through the shades.

Fugitive Laughter

I visit Good Hope Lutheran Church
with friend Sylva where Reverend Hammer
pounds his sermon, words bouncing
off stained glass like frantic doves,
as if those windows, leaded with outlines
of saints, were all that separated this flock
from heaven. But amid the theatrics
of his skyward delivery, the backdrop
of morning sun flickering through cobalt
and crimson panes—stilted saints
caught in eternal poses of rapt attention,
I glimpse the congregation pewed in rows,
straight lines straddling heaven and hell.
The attention morphs to a tension that snaps—
takes me to funny, and funny becomes
contagious, my shoulders, then Sylva's
rising and falling. Even as we try to shackle
our urge to release unbridled laughter,
it rolls forth from our deepest cells,
winged, and beyond salvation.

Quiet Rooms

In Chicago we stay at Hotel Sax, across from
House of Blues, ambience informed by a faint
harmonica grieving about loss. A silhouette

of a vintage chandelier silk-screened on the wall
of our room, the wallpaper, hip velvet flock without
the velvet, elegant curtains the color of airplane silver—

the past wants to be remembered. In the lounge we sip
aperitifs made of rare elderflower liqueur. Expensive
but lacking the fabric of a cocktail. Sugar and water,

barely a hint of floral except for a gold and purple pansy
floating like a bruised moon. *When Sunny Gets Blue*
moans from a sax, penetrating as a human voice.

A three-tiered earring, Mona Lisa's eye, regal crown,
skull and crossbones, dangles from the earlobe
of a woman sitting alone, next to me. Another riff

about the now of then. Outside the hotel,
a sweet-looking husky man asks for spare change.
He doesn't pretend to be hungry for food. I want to

donate anyway. My husband says he's an addict,
just going to use it to get high. I say we're all addicted
to some euphoria, the daggered edges of love—

l and *v* tucked beside pillowed curves of *o* and *e*—
a place to rest with one eye open. Hard to be alone
holding the long note knowing somewhere

there's a call and response—horn from a distant
freighter, train whistle late at night, song for
quiet rooms, and the blues that won't let you forget.

Agoraphobia Contrapuntal

A sheltered life can be a very daring life, for all serious daring starts from within.

EUDORA WELTY

The house is your captor
a thorny nest,
where birds unhinge
haunting incantations
outside these rooms
you bargain with yourself
today you'll walk a few yards
another continent
your heart crescendos
you quake with tremors
don't look back
locked in Grandma's closet
the walls close in
you need to see the sky
beyond your Van Gogh *Starry Night*

you can't ignore
the hermit thrushes
their fluted songs
like traffic's listless serenade
that lull you hostage
one foot out, now the other
to the mailbox
just there
in the thinning air
you feel like crawling
remember how
your body, curled like a fist
the door, a dark mouth
come out, it's safe
beyond your light bulb moon.

Finding Fathers

1

After my father left, the lights dimmed
until I saw the glow of a gooseneck
across the street. Our neighbor, a professor,
kept the side door open and I'd let myself in,
sit quietly in the basement corner absorbing
the comfort of scents: journals and pencils,
coffee and corduroy. He was a Rembrandt
bathed in chiaroscuro, hunched over stacks
of papers, piles of books—a scholar of distant
lands. On occasion he'd smile and nod,
but I sensed he didn't really see me, here
in this subterranean chapel where I worshipped
men who need to wander, learned that even
a cozy room can be a wilderness for one.

2

My uncle wanted me to be a tomboy,
the son he didn't have. I caught fly balls,
hard balls, fast balls that whooshed by
at what, 65 miles an hour? When one punched
me in the solar plexus, sure, I fell, clutching
my stomach like a girl, but I managed
to wave, *It's okay, I'm okay.* And when
he said, you're fine, suck it up—I did.

3

At first Dr. M wanted to adopt me,
but then he wanted to marry me. We ate
oysters and snails, filet and frog legs,
traveled where the lights were brighter—
Aztec pyramids, Vegas shows. But I was
happy staying in, listening to *The Tales
of Hoffman*, the poet who falls in love
with Olympia, daughter of a clever inventor.

Hoffman is unaware the girl is one of his
inventions, a mechanical doll who sings and dances.
She slows down now and then, has to be rewound,
but Hoffman is so in love he doesn't notice.

4
My father used a fancy fountain pen,
sent postcards from around the world
always in his trademark green ink.
I'd think of him when I looked at herbs
and evergreens, lawns and chestnut trees—
even after the grass had yellowed,
the leaves had fallen.

Postcards of Home and Homesick

I'm lounging in my Detroit yard
listening to Chopin, eating a peach.

> The City of Lights was shadowed
> by the Carpathian Mountains—
> a Baltic breeze did little to soothe
> his ache of home. His postcards—
> polonaises and mazurkas—
> *cannons hidden among roses.*

The peach smells like a nocturne.
I hold the pit, planting a tree
in my palm, imagining the soil
where roots travel and tendrils reach.

> His music: ballads and preludes,
> waltzes and etudes, notes
> forming the music of exile,
> sound of a thousand footsteps
> marching home.

I envy how roots trust darkness,
taproot, heart root, burrowing
through layers of silt and clay,
tunneling through bedrock
to anchor a home.

> Chopin asked that his Paris grave
> be scattered with Polish soil, wanted
> his heart returned to Warsaw.
> His sister carried its red bloom
> in a glass urn, a rose crawling up
> the picket fence of childhood.

I've planted my heart in my yard,
anchored to the soil of home,
the place I first felt the sun, my face
always turning in that direction.

Childhood Revisited as a Musical

Debussy's *Claire de Lune* and me
     lying beneath an oak in the yard
searching beyond the nest

of branches that I might discover
     something personal in the sky
not the storm riding in on an easterly,

but my grandmother, Sittu—*Ride of the Valkyries*,
     a woman who's been taught to worship
the men in our family with the reverence

of Handel's *Messiah*, and me—*Bombastes
     Furioso*, a tragic comic opera—not for
my humor, more my DNA—girl not to be

encouraged. In the farce the men shoot
     each other over a woman. Then stand
to do it again for applause. I was shooting

for *My Fair Lady*, damsel in new dress,
     All I want is a room somewhere . . .
knowing Sitto would sooner lock me up

than send this Liza Doolittle to the ball—
     Yet there were times she abandoned
her chorus of fates and furies. Saturday nights

when the theme from *I Love Lucy*
     filled the room, I watched her drop her mask
of tragedy, laugh with burlesque abandon, covering

her mouth to suppress her natural impulse.
     Let me en-ter-tain you, let me make you smile—
the *Gypsy* inside aching to sing out.

Dreams of My Father

He hugs me and weeps,
says he has fallen in love
with a woman named Myra

and shows me her snapshot
pasted inside the top of an old
candy tin. In the photo she is five,

riding her tricycle,
I think it reminds him
of me! His car is loaded

with bags of sugar. Everything
he needs to bake cookies, to live on.
I don't question any of it.

The bags look like pillows. I tell him
I haven't been able to find
a comfortable one. My sleep

is restless, has been since he left.
He draws my head to his chest.
I can't move. It's softer

than anything I've known.
I tell him I've become
a vine with tangled roots.

Something inside me cannot
take to the soil. I tell him
I've lain my head on grass

and tree, book and desk,
seashore and window ledge—
all of it a window ledge.

Lost on the Champs-Élysées

My Father—I never learned his habits,
his mannerisms. Later, when
he was almost a stranger, except
for the word *father* which I defined as
postcards in green ink, he took me,
my brother, and Mother, whom he'd
fought to win back all these years,
to Paris. I watched him sip champagne,
something he was unaccustomed to,
trying to show her he'd become

more flexible, more fun. His portly
body bobbled as he skipped down the
Champs-Élysées like the child I was
before he left. I turned to my mother
and though I thought I'd measured
every nuance of her expressions,
deciphered every cue—this was different,
a look of embarrassment, disgust, one
that, in that moment, estranged
me from my parents and left me
orphaned from myself.

La Vie en Gris

I drive home from work on this cold spring day,
minivan window framing the world's familiar footage,
and I imagine I'm in a Truffaut film. The sun cuts
through gray clouds—a spotlight. Movie score—
the radio playing music sultry as Piaf's voice.

And the protagonist, a girl who wants too much,
wishes she could smoke French cigarettes and spend
long afternoons lingering over crusty baguettes slathered
with full-cream *fromage*. She sips goblets of Bordeaux
with her lover, Jean-Claude something-or-other
who brings the wildflowers she loves because

they never need tending to. He kisses
the back of her neck—*baisers volés*, stolen kisses,
his voice sexy as Icart's *Illusion*, and whispers,
"Je t'adore ma chérie, ma *petite* chérie." Her eyes
close, charmeuse curtains hiding what she doesn't

want to see—or hear. Don't say dirty dishes,
deadlines—or diet. *Oh mon dieu*, not diet! Well,
if you must, say it to that ache of French music
that makes even sadness seem pretty. Because
she doesn't want to leave, but it's time to go. Say,
"*every-sing* will be okay, *Amour*." Say it again.

Reconsidering Yellow

She obsessed as if she were a pantoum, repeating the first
and third lines of her life. For a while she was unsure
of the first so she improvised, deciding between:

The girl with curls skipped blithely in the sun-dotted
dress her father bought in Venezuela. Or: *Children*
who are mistreated often choose a life of crime.

The third line she took from Josephine Hart's book,
Damage. "Damaged people are dangerous. They know
they can survive." Though it wasn't clear to whom

they are dangerous until she researched gray areas
for psych about suicide being homicide turned inward,
and vice versa. Her father left when she was seven,

dislodging her inner compass and triggering fear
of abandonment. It was as if every road faded to black,
prompting her to define agoraphobia as: Best to stay put

should he ever return. For the second line, she referred to
a passage from Gibran's *Prophet:* "Your children
are not your children; they are the sons and daughters

of life's longing for itself." This inspired her to consider
brighter colors, study art history, and write: *When I was young,*
I hated yellow / but after carrying the sea on my back, /

blue weighed me down and I realized how heavy / salt really is.
It meant she chose hunger over thirst and admired big-
shouldered men. Unfortunately, her line, *I licked the salt*

from every animal to find the taste of you again added extra
weight mid stanza. Later, it was all about maps and manners.
Please and *Thank You* this. *Fuck You* that. She imagined

dining with Prince Charles after reading about
the importance of etiquette at their dinner table.
She hated the cacophony of clinking spoon

against melamine plate, could never imagine herself
at a noodle bar in Japan. The slurping, she thought,
might cause her to pick up an errant chopstick and insert it

into someone's left ventricle. It happened at family dinners—
the urge, especially when serving fresh tomato marinara
over capellini al dente. End stanza. She was through with red.

If you dine with the queen there are rules. Once Her Majesty
finishes, all forks down . . . it's a long list. Point is, the girl
could not wrap her mind around purple as a symbol for blue

bloods, though it made sense as the bruised metaphor for black
sheep. Familial tension forced her on all fours one Christmas,
crawling around Aunt Emma's violet shag to the beat

of tachycardia during a full-blown panic attack. This, after
her brother Todd breaks one of Auntie's antique goblets,
then deliberately cuts his hand on a shard before Mother

could scold him. Segue from sacrificial lamb trope
to impromptu alliteration: sinner, suffering, stigmata.
By the last stanza the girl reconsiders yellow, a color

she's come to regard as the bright subtext of her pantoumesque
journey, that which repeats—like the circles on the sun-dotted
dress her father brought back from Venezuela.

When You Cannot Sleep

you measure nuances in the sky,
black turns indigo with a gradient
of air-force blue gone navy,
and the full moon fades
as you play connect the dots
with random stars

when you cannot sleep

you feel a kinship with those
who share your circadian rhythm,
refer to Edison who slept only
two hours, and Martha Stewart four,
which explains why she has time
to raise llamas, and blue egg
chickens, and why he invented
the light bulb

when you cannot sleep

you test the remedies
for insomnia —chamomile tea,
warm milk, hot bath— placing
your bed in the ideal feng shui
spot—further from the door
or diagonally from the door,
but not in line with the door

when you cannot sleep

you replay the day, the week,
your entire life—turning to
Facebook, reading every post
going back five years, realizing
how desperate you are when
you find yourself taking the

*What Fairy Tale Character
Are You?* quiz

when you cannot sleep

you entertain moving
to the other side of the equator
convinced you're a victim
of the time zone or daylight
savings time or leap year

when you cannot sleep

you become foolishly hopeful
as you approach your
800-thread-count sheets—
wearing 100% Egyptian cotton,
having tried the Serta Perfect,
Tempur-Pedic, Kingsdown,
ready to mortgage your home
for the $60,000 Vividus
and the promise of *sleeping
on a cloud.*

Foreboding Frog

I've always suspected that insomnia
is really the fear of death. And confirmed it
last night when during a rare REM sleep
a frog stalked me through a barren
landscape. Just me, and the frog. As it
inched closer, I turned to scare it away—
the frog kept coming. From a distance it shone
bud green. But as it leapt forth it grew larger,
turning brown as a dead leaf skating on the whims
of the wind. I tried to mow down the towering
toad, hurling stones in a David and Goliath
battle, shouting, Go away damn frog!
Then I realized— even before I woke up,
before I had a chance to anoint the dream
with reason, that a mortal in a boundless
desert pleading with a giant frog, will hear
only its inevitable reply—croak, croak, croak.

Physics for Dummies

She couldn't fall asleep, had watched a program
    on PBS about string theories, branes, parallel
        universes, atom smashing, gravity versus

electromagnetic forces. All right, it wasn't as if
    she understood these theories— additional
        dimensions beyond the three

she and most everyone are familiar with:
    up and down, side to side, back and forth—
        she had trouble fitting all that motion

into her day as it was, more strings
    than she needed. There were days she
        wished she could downshift molecularly,

maybe live in the country or on an island,
    but that could be boring as hell, might *be* hell,
        no visceral stimulation, the cortisol rush

she craves, is addicted to. She remembered
    the outer limits of agoraphobia, how even
        that might relate to these string etc., theories—

dimensions of time and space—up and down
    was fine, side to side, okay, but back and forth
        was problematic. Her dimensions

had morphed to two and yeah she knew she needed
    the third, but there was a time when even a photo
        of a lone figure paddling across a river,

red canoe against a Vermont blue sky
    caused anxiety—and if those physics professors
        on PBS had been watching they might have

associated the ripples in the river
  with the reverberations of her nerves,
    might have asked what she was afraid of

and she would have answered, "Heights
  but horizontal instead of vertical," and those brainy
    men, some with skinny bodies because they eat,

sleep, and drink science. Some with shocks
  of white hair that resemble conductors
    for electromagnetic forces—they might have

thought these fears were strange, of another
  universe, but one she understood as
    parallel when her father left before

she could tell him about the gravity
  of gravity, the heart gone alien, and how time
    and space can become infinitesimal,

which might explain why she would question
  theories beyond her reach, on a night when
    the stars grow too faint to notice.

Mr. Right

Best if his head resembles
a planet, his face worldly
with a curious physiognomy.
His eyes should be celestial
as asteroids that have traveled
and landed, possessing a knowledge
of trajectories, the gathering of particles,
the passing of time. Let his voice project
a sonorous tenor, not the gravitas of a bass
but something resonant as the hum
of a growing tree. His character
should be ethereal, not the halo
of an angel, more layered
like rings of Saturn. His heart—a Mars,
close enough to see but far enough
to be romantic. Best if his arms
reach like oceans careening
to shores, and the lines of his palms
be maps to other moons. His nature
should be inquisitive—the temperament
of a theoretical physicist about to discover
what makes us tick, a constellation
of intellect and bewilderment—
the vulnerability of surprise.

Falling in Love at the Speed of the *William Tell* "Overture"

Love at first sight: in French, *un coup*
de foudre, strike of a thunderbolt,
in Spanish, *flechazo*, an arrow shot.
But I call it Neanderthal, Big Apple
bang, chemical badaboom. Take
a Detroit girl with her notion
of Prince Perfect: urbane but irreverent,
smart but makes her feel smarter. A man
who knows the apple is a member of
the rose family. Add funny valentine
who says I love you in no less
than six languages. Or, cut to

rough-around-the-edges
New Yorker, cute guy who says
fuggedaboudit in Brooklynese.
One who gives her a rose
on their first date, Sweetest day,
and before she can say lickety-split,
casts a spell that renders her
silly as a nitrous oxide overdose.
Put said rose on desk and notice
instead of fading, it grows brighter.
Begin to suspect it's because deep
reflective sighs have displaced
the ecosphere with a chemical
flight that causes her to swan
around as if her head has more helium
than matter. Forget sleep— even sugar
loses its luster to make way
for sensory deprivation needed
to relive every moment spent with him
who has absconded with her brain,
a boing on the noggin, Newtonian clunk—
a hi-yo here we go, away!

An Orgasm Is a Terrible Thing to Waste

In Klimt's *Lovers*, you see a moment just before the kiss, eyes locked,
steam rising to form foreboding clouds. Klimt had a thing for working

in his silk robe—au natural. I imagine him painting *The Kiss*, couple
draped in gilded mosaic on the edge of a flowered cliff, world dissolving

around them. But in *Lovers*, cloud demons drift overhead: hags,
dead people, threatening mother-figures watching. Picture Woody Allen's

Oedipus Wrecks. His mother, with the voice of Betty Boop, hovers over
Sheldon—literally. During a freak accident at a magic show she vanishes,

becomes a cloud hanging over Manhattan like a Macy's parade float,
announcing to crowds below things like *Sheldon was a bed-wetter*. The only

way to bring her down is to break up with his goyishe fiancée, marry the nice
Jewish girl. Reminds me of my father wanting to send me to Lebanon

to betroth me to a good Druze boy. But my aunt had a loveless arranged
marriage, Grandma was married off at 12, Mother at 15. And since I already

had a boyfriend and Auntie had become a lover of romance novels, she
coached me to say *eat shit* in Arabic, which sent the Druze boy running.

The boy waiting in Michigan, the one I was in love with, at first it was just
the two of us, but back then, and even now during intimate moments

with my husband, sometimes the room clouds up with ghosts of relatives past.
Last week my friend Mary blushed when she told me her Catholic

conscience kept her from unleashing "certain things." And like her I'm not
inclined to go into detail about canoodling, though I too enjoy being naked

under the robe, as it were. Still, I can't watch *Show Dogs* on TV
when the owners seem to take pleasure watching their bitches hump

for the camera. And I find it fascinating even now, that my hands
are falling asleep— numb at the keyboard—but not before I mention

an article on fish genitalia, how males with large sex organs are more likely
to get mates but also more likely to be eaten by predators.

Punch Drunk Love
—after the movie

A loner, prone to fits of rage, he lies on top,
his nose an inch away from hers, says,
"I want to smash your face, it's so pretty

I want to smash it with a sledge hammer."
There's a long pause. Her eyes searching
as if to reach inside him. And I'm afraid

of what she'll find, until I realize she heard it as
Your face is unbearably pretty. I'm scared of
of the way it makes me feel. I watch his

reaction when she says "I want to scoop out
your eyes and eat them." How he hears
I love the way I see myself in you, I want that

inside me. They kiss like ice cubes melting
in Scotch, and I remember what it means
to be invisible, wandering the city,

an outsider even my mother never knew.
I walk down Grand River Avenue
along the Redford cemetery, a ghost

who cannot hide the scent that stray dogs
chase, the mix of fear and tough from
tramping in wilderness too big to mark.

In the movie they're drawn to
each other like plastic kissing dolls—
as if each had been looking for

the other without knowing—and
I see myself — heart with the teeth
of a dog that never means to bite.

Touching the Wound

The man in the movie who brings her almond croissants,
still warm—the one who orders foie gras and figs stuffed
with Roquefort, I watch him become more attractive

with his description of a veal shank: the marrow infusing
broth, reduced to a rich, unctuous sauce for osso bucco.
He isn't handsome until he speaks, and I follow

her eyes widening, her brow rising like heat as he folds
her into the warmth of his passion. He's not after a dish
that merely seduces, he wants full body with authentic notes—

wants to discern, describe until she can taste his words.
It reminds me of the poet who wrote, "The Knife Accuses
the Wound," a woman who knows the argument

of the knife, that sometimes wounds are an invitation—
tender lips that speak of a desire to hold onto that which
is familiar,even when it hurts. The man is steadfast,

he wants this woman, one who's never been nurtured
by a mother, or a considerate lover yet still has an appetite
for life. He's drawn to her complexity, like wine

that takes on the flavor of the barrel as it ages, or
the way a woman who may not be a beauty can be
beautiful and you just want to be with her.

He understands the subtleties of trust, how
touching the wound will remind her that it's there.
How only then can it be forgotten.

Last Night I Dreamed
I Stole the Croissants

I was stealing in French,

stole tender crescents
with a translucent glaze,
crusty and raspberry filled,

stole light
clouds of pastry
layered with butter,

glistening like Antoinette's baubles.

I stole the moon, I stole la lune,
took le voyage dans la lunette.

I was the cow, la vache qui rit,
laughing and buoyant in flight.

I stole the sea, la mer, and la *feesh*,
that jump and dance in the moonlight.

I stole the night and the stars,
and wrapped them in silver
shaped like the neck of a swan . . .

Oh, don't be jaloux, cher,

don't foofaraw like blue jays
and chimps. (They can become
jealous too.)

It was only one night
(cinq minutes dans ma coeur),

and, *oui*, some oozed
with chocolate,

sadly, none ever touched my lips.

Power of Suggestion

I

Beyond all reason I reach
for another body-basting
carbo deluxe—ethereal
profiteroles filled with crème
de la moo, drizzled in plump
threads of chocolate, "*good
chocolate*" says the slender
TV cook, drowsy-eyed, drunk
with anticipation. She says
anyone can bake like a French chef.
I think I heard her say, "You too,
Diane," the soft applause
of sugar spilling into the pot,
crystals bronzed by the heat.
Caramel is easy, resisting is hard.

2

I walked the dog yesterday
in freezing temperatures,
bright sun beckoning, a warming
sheild against the toothy wind—
the world gone virgin white,
blingified landscape of stark
extravagance. A mid-winter
craving this Harry Winston
shimmer on loan—raw glitter,
flawless crystals, and Figaro
pawing through like
it was just snow.

Happy-Go-Lucky

You know that dream where you sit in your car
and the seat automatically moves forward
to the perfect position? The car starts itself
driving you places you've never been and talks to you
about your worries with that calm, yet commanding
OnStar voice? You confide that people don't love you
as much as you'd like them to, and if they did,
you wouldn't, couldn't possibly, return that much
love anyway. This reminds you of a movie line,
"Love itself is what's left over after being in love
is burned away." Then the voice says, "Love can be
a confusing state of mind." And a map full of states
appears on the GPS screen—not Utah, or Michigan,
but a New-York-state-of-mind which you've acquired
even though you're from Detroit. Because you identify
with people who wear a lot of black and who enjoy
a frenetic, somewhat impersonal subway, graffiti,
melting pot sensibility—along with those delicious
ethnic dishes. And you think maybe, just maybe,
the car will stop at a good Provençal restaurant
or mahogany paneled steakhouse where they serve
bone marrow, now that you're no longer embarrassed
to say you like it. Especially since Anthony Bourdain
posed naked holding a huge soup bone over his
"meatballs," saying he loves the high cholesterol stuff.
"But," the voice cautions," "he drinks too much, and eats
things that could change your nature." Change your nature?
What does that mean? I can't go there. Though I sense
the need for turn-by-turn navigation when the melodic
OnStar voice says, "Love isn't really all that complicated—
it's the fear of love that snookers us."Reminds me
of the time it took me days to untangle an impossible
wad of necklaces, knotted chains of my own doing.
And the fortune cookie I once got that said,
"you are about to eat a fortune cookie—"
how once in a while even destiny takes a shortcut.

To Lean

Having injured
my shoulder
I dream
of racing
down the Thames,
part of a crew,
sixteen-oared ,
octuple scull,
long slender shell,
symmetrical,
keelless
feet fixed
seats glide,
lock and socket,
stiff-armed
sweep of oars—
lift of water,
bracing
smooth—
a lubricant
to be part of
this synchrony,
able to lean
on others, ride
the breastbone
of a bird,
without wings or
even a feather.

Thinking about What Matters

Because I just won a million British pounds
according to the e-mail from a stranger—like
pop-ups that flash while I'm googling a recipe
from the next great chef, to inform me I've won

a fabulous vacation to a tundra, or glacial forest.
Truth is I'd like to win wings, Newtonian wings.
Now that's a prize, along with a ticket for time

travel. Would like to know firsthand what it's like
to send postcards from a parallel universe.
At last, I'd have coffee with the physicists

I admire—my treat. For there is no one more
attentive than a scientist who explores everything
that isn't nailed down, the no-gravity zone,

solar wind—particles invisible to the naked eye.
And wouldn't they be surprised, wouldn't I
be the belle of the String Theory Ball if I could

wax poetic on probabilities and decoherence—
shine a light at the end of the big bang tunnel.
Because when it comes to trips, nothing compares

to the journey of what-if, and imagine how,
nothing transports . . . well, except perhaps
the incomparable service at The Peninsula Hotel,

and come to think of it, the breakfast
at Norma's in Le Parker Meridian—the chef
is a culinary genius. But beyond that—

nothing comes close to gazing up
at the beguiling cosmos, knowing
there is more, infinitely more.

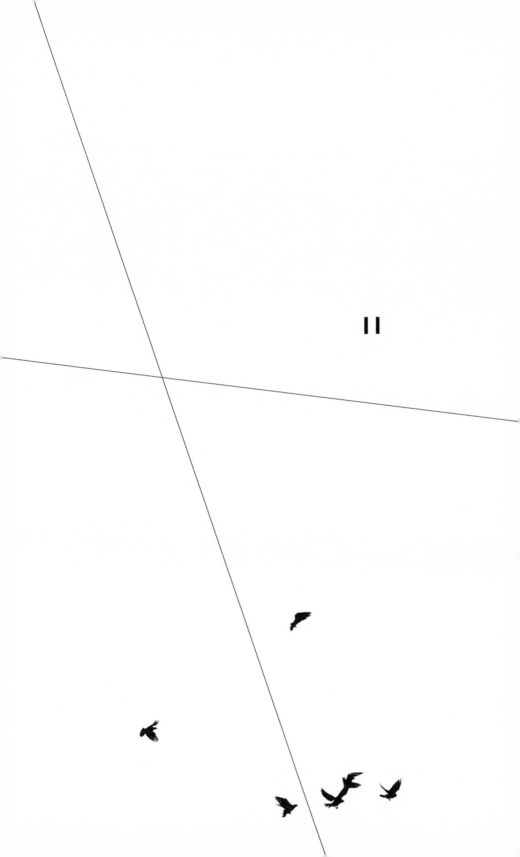

II

Milk

I loved to watch my grandmother boil milk,
turn the soft curd hard to make yogurt

she called *leban*. She poured it, steaming,
into a green ceramic bowl to cool, dipping

her finger to test for the right temperature
before adding spoonfuls of culture saved

from the last batch. It cooled with a sweet, thin
layer of skin, *cowshie,* a delicacy she'd skim

from the surface, give to me before blanketing
the bowl like a newborn until it set. In her village,

girls were not coddled. Married off at 12, twice
divorced by 40, she resented the men she left behind.

I became a reminder of what she never had, what might
have been. Some days she was bitter as raw olives,

threatening to boil the girl out of me. Her face red
as the blush she hated to see me wear—*Sharmuta!*

she'd shout, *whorrre!* making sure I understood.
My lip-glossed lips pursed tight, coat hiding sexier

outfits tucked into my waistband that bulged like
the bump of pregnant women. Women she mocked,

made fun of. But in the warmth of her kitchen I got a taste
of the mothering she gave my brother—less of

the ambivalence that made me cautious as one who
carefully tastes an open bottle of milk, just as it begins

to spoil—testing for that edge that yields a residue
of sugar—before the acid aftertaste.

Without Child

There are stories I tell my family,
my friends—but I imagine they're not

the story I'd tell a child, sitting at the side
of her bed, the room softly lit, portrait

of the two of us under a cherry tree,
posing on a carpet of white blossoms.

I see myself telling her how beautiful she was
the first time I saw her, imagine her sweet scent,

her eyes, penetrating and wise with
a thousand answers to what I've questioned

about matters of the heart. She reaches for my hand,
the strength of her grip surprising, frightening—

the attachment, an offering of love
I couldn't take or give. Once I held a baby,

sat her on the deep lap of memory,
and tucked her in, until we both forgot.

Room Full of Children Staring at Me

1

The Vietnamese manicurist
asks me how many children I have.
She must think I'm God or Buddha,
able to answer what is unknowable.

2

I never stop wondering what it would have been
like to connect with the searching eyes of infant,
to find some version of myself in them.
Some days it's endless speculation, other
days, simple as the girl who wasn't there
when they handed out the word *mother*.

3

It's a mystery, a dime novel.
I'm the heroine who's travelled
to a remote island in search of
the stolen formula sealed in a vault
inside an unmarked catacomb.
My flashlight works, but oh clever villain,
just as I uncoil the delicate parchment,
alas, the disappearing ink.

4

There it is, the age you don't recognize,
time of ripe fruit falling—when the body
can no longer wait for the heart to catch up.

5

How many ways are there
to ruin a child? Tie them to you,
teach them to trust only your words,
speak your thoughts. Abandon them,
give them too much freedom,

make it hard to follow the long
scent home. Lie. Not the good
lies but the ones that keep them
from themselves. Train them
to be the little parents until
they're tired and weary
of having to mother again.

6
The word for a woman who bears a child is mother.
What is the word for a woman who does not?

The Grammar of Memory

A young girl, my grandmother Sittu looks out her window
at the mountain in her Lebanese village. She describes it: soft purple,
yellow and gold—a smear of fig jam on warm buttered toast.

She knows the nature of mountains, how they change, respond
to the sky—to seasons that move in and out with the freedom
of migrating birds. And how it blocks her view, how the road

there stops abruptly, a period at the end of a sentence. She never
imagined one day her son, deaf from an accident, would find a job
cracking rocks on the gravel path near their home, stacking them

to build houses for others, a life for himself. How he would read lips,
the onslaught of words we simply listen for, how image by image
he would decipher the lilt of voices, the exclamation points,

question marks. Sittu knows what it means to be cut off, forbidden
to speak her mind, even to learn to read and write. She learns
too soon how to be a woman—so early, she can't remember

being a child. In my suburban Detroit home, I curl up in bed,
my body a comma, punctuating the passage of one day to the next.
I read stories and poems, read for both of us the way I used to

read to her after school, watching the indelible mountain
inside her diminish in her eyes. It's said we sleep
to improve our recall, to remember the big moments,

but also to get rid of minutiae that would overwhelm us—
our brain editing what it doesn't need—the brief encounters,
the wilting of wildflowers, the dark clouds.

Arranged Marriage
—for Sittu

Imagine climbing
an almond tree,
groping your way
among its pink
blossoms,
you straddle
limbs thin
as your
delicate arms,
your legs
wobbly
as a newborn
lamb's.
You are twelve
reaching
for the ear
of the sky
from the top
of this tree
hoping to
be heard
by any God
on this, your
wedding day,
a young Eve,
taking refuge,
dreading
the much older
Adam who
celebrates
below,
oblivious
to the hard
bark that
scrapes

your soft
flesh,
flesh whiter
than a woman's,
white as
the new
bed linens
that mouth
your name
below.

Yellow According to Rilke

The towering maple in the yard
woke me at 3 a.m. Its leaves turned

bombastic yellow—overnight.
The glow, a Galileo globe

filling my room, as if the moon,
like an impetuous lover,

had drawn closer,
                    was all mine.

I stayed awake thinking I should train
my body to age like this tree, its blaze

of Thomas's *rage against the dying of the light*—
train to be the eyes of Blake's tiger burning bright.

Rilke said, *There is only a single urgent task:*
to attach oneself someplace to nature,

to that which is strong, striving and bright.

It's the way he saw Cézanne's citrus—Baroque,
sculptural, indestructible in their stubbornness.

O yellow of lemons—make that *limoni*,
            (sounds even more yellow in Italian).

O honeyed stars, tonight you are
                    la luna bell ringing,
                        the yolk heart sunny-side up.

Who can sleep in a world with so much yellow?

Artemisia Absinthium

I look out the window, wonder if this French
liqueur has influenced the way I see the leaves
sprouting from baby green to sage adolescence—
the color of risk & knowing. Absinthe: bitter

wormwood of silvery leaves and nodding
flowers. Blend aromatic fennel, star anise,
juniper, and dittany. Add lemon balm,
angelica, hyssop, coriander and macerate

until narcotic green. Van Gogh poured
its color onto canvas, thick impastos of ochre
and emerald spilling into *The Night Café*.
Hemingway, Wilde, Poe, and Baudelaire

reached for its ripe graphic fruit, a prickly
essence prodding openings for poems
and stories. The leaves in my yard
flutter like café awnings. I imagine

Lautrec, his hollow cane filled with
absinthe, its heady anise perfume—
Gauguin driven by it to make his colors
bolder. Artists and poets gathering

for the green hour. Picasso lifts his glass,
*If only we could pull out our brains
and use only our eyes*, toasting *La Fée Verte*,
nymph who makes his wish come true.

Weeping Women

Picasso dipped his brush in their tears—
long, deliberate strokes
saturated with salt, agony.

I walked around with boxes
of Kleenex, reams of toilet paper.
Told anyone who would listen
that you left me.

They could not paint their misery
and so they wrote about it,
pens weeping the blue ink of loss.

I wasn't embarrassed by my tears.
I told a salesman, confided
in strangers, people in bookstores,
where I'd sit in the self-help section for hours.

They wrote how their bodies emptied
became mere outlines, white doves
with hearts dangling from their beaks.

I fell asleep holding books that might help me
hate you. The waitress in the Chinese restaurant
who didn't speak English, understood. Colleagues
came to accept the wail and hum, the sounds
my body made to let me know I was still alive.

They wrote how he abandoned
one for another—how he wanted Dora
to watch him tell his new love Françoise
that *she* was his most beautiful muse.

The rain of grief continued to fall,
I feared I would drown.

He painted their teeth
sharp and jagged,
their broken hunger.

> But I loved the part of me without defenses
> that didn't think of humiliation or fashion,
> the hunter who'd lick the salt of every animal
> to find the taste of you again.

Cubist Still Life

Her parents named her
    Cubist Still Life,
addressed her from different angles,
    taught her to ignore barriers
of time and space.
    But Cubist had challenges
in school, failed
    to use proper punctuation
having been accustomed to hearing
    everything simultaneously,
and in a single sentence.
    She grew sullen in adolescence,
wore drab beiges and browns.
    Her yearbook described her
as ambiguous, shallow, and one most likely
    to collect dust. She suffered knowing
she was viewed as one dimensional,
    all at once, from every angle—
that people thought they knew
    all there was to know about her.
Cubist rebelled, hung out with Impressionists,
    painted her rhomboid rooms
in sunlight-dappled pastels— a passing fancy.
    She dated a Fauvist, wore intense
color, defining her edges in thick
    kohl-black lines. But it was
Abstract Expressionist who showed her
    how to improvise, find her true essence,
urged her to embrace her angular visage.
    Cubist became known for her smart style,
wore collage embellished with words
    and textures. Friends began to notice
her aura of mystery and complex depth.
    In the end, she became a crusader
for truth and inner beauty, praised for allowing
    others to see the world more fully.

Origami Pantoum

If I fold a book of poetry to hang on the wall,
tuck the corner of a page into the crease,
fold the top of the next just the same way,
will the words fall out as I walk by?

Fold the corner of a page into the crease where
Lehman's sky crumbles, a million paper dots,
will the words fall out, hang in the air,
float into Li-Young's wife's braided hair?

Lehman's sky crumbling, a million paper dots
changing the season from autumn to winter,
floating in Li-Young's wife's braided hair
like a thousand cranes landing on Oliver's branches.

Changing the season from autumn to winter,
Whitman sings songs amid cold leaves of grass,
a thousand cranes gather on Oliver's branch,
she's lonely as a lover who's decided to leave.

Whitman sings songs amid cold leaves of grass,
Stevens sees a blackbird only half a dozen ways.
Lonely as a lover who's decided to leave,
Basho's like a butterfly bereft on the moor.

Stevens sees a blackbird only three ways now,
something Chekhovian is happening here,
Basho is dreaming on a steep, withered moor,
Neruda's saddest line runs into his happiest.

Something Chekhovian is happening here,
fanning this poem into form's measured call,
will Neruda's saddest line find Dunn's Happiness,
if I fold a book of poetry to hang on the wall?

Looking for Stephen Dunn

You tell us not to write about what we really love,
are close to. Too much at stake. The *fictive*, you say,
adds interest. But then you say,

> *finally the personal is all that matters,*
> *we spend years describing stones,*
> *chairs, abandoned farmhouses—*
> *until we're ready.*

Well, I think I'm ready. That is to say,
I'm in love with you. I discovered this
at your last reading. Sure, you're balding,

a little pudgy in the Pulitzer—dressed
in classic white shirts, and professorial
vests. But I know I'm not alone when
I say the way you recite your poetry
is sexy.

> *And the unwritten caption*
> *that to be wild means nothing you do*
> *or have done needs to be explained.*

I could imagine walking up to you,
throwing down your *New & Selected*,
and taking you to an abandoned farmhouse
where I'd show you some of my best

metaphors. You may say I'm not ready,
that it's a mistake to force a facile connection
between art and life. But until then,

> *I think I'll keep on describing things*
> *to ensure that they really happened.*

Body Language

In a dream my friend who's drawn
to elegance, wears a white cotton
tank top, not her usual silk and lace.
Her body has been tattooed, not in dragons

or fireflies but fancy fonts in basic black,
fonts with more flourish than *Lucida
Calligraphy*—but nothing so garish
as **ALGERIAN** or obvious as *Blackadder*.

I see the word Poetry, the *Palace Script*
of a *P* swanning around her arm
as if the artist were listening
to Tchaikovsky while inking her flesh,

and it reminds me of the young
Asian girl whose father, a calligrapher,
wrote the story of creation on her face
each year for her birthday. When she grew

older, she could only fall in love
with a man who wanted her to write
on his body, and he on hers.
They scrawled love poems in Arabic:

I pass by these walls,
the walls of Layla / And I kiss
this wall and that wall . . .
It's been said that we are all

the characters in our dreams—
the graffiti artist, the calligrapher,
the girl who knows nothing is indelible
except for what's written on the heart.

I am the one who scribbles promises
with eyebrow pencil on my lover's skin,
the heat of our bodies melting the tip
faster than I can write.

Lee Miller's Father

photographed her in the nude
as a girl and beyond. Developing
in the dark room, the emulsion:

silver halide grains, cells forming
a gelatin layer. What daughter can resist
the filial spotlight. Flash that puts

everything out of focus. Those fetching
images, their latitude for exposure
stained and sensitized the surface.

Posing became her paradigm
for love, remoteness the damage
she bore *in matters of sentiment.*

A fashion model for *Vogue,*
journalist on the war front,
a colleague snapped her bathing

in Hitler's tub, the Führer's framed
picture on the ledge, a classical
sculpture opposite. The newspapers

ran it, labeling her inscrutable as ever,
"A woman caught between horror
and beauty." It's been said this lack

of sensitivity ended her career. But not
before she shot Buchenwald and Dachau,
bodies piled high as the wall inside her.

Her knack for distance allowing her
to get close to the dead, blur the line
between captor and captive.

Phantom Limbs

Missing me one place search another

WALT WHITMAN

My friend's husband
lost his leg. She calls it
a tease of the worst order,
the way it causes you
to keep re-losing the limb.

The body parts
with parts of itself,
but the mind insists
they're still there.
You feel
the itch, twitch,
a gesture
when speaking.

Wound dresser
during the war, Whitman
heard soldiers' cries
of limbs returning,
*the mind stalking
the flesh.* He read

poetry, tried to heal
*what the surgeon
couldn't touch,
our deepest remains.*

I swear my arms grow
shorter when loved ones
leave—phantom
father, absent friend

there just out of reach,
like some untouchable
bird that flutters inside.

Nest

I

What if I build a nest
from the stillness
between breath held
and breath released?

What if I build my nest
with the fevered breeze
of a paper fan? Or titian

strands from a floating
sunset. What if I can't feel
my heart but feel the strands
knitting around it?

Is wilting a surrender
to earth's nest—
or generosity?
What if I build my nest
from the fiber of a flower
that has lost suppleness
but retains the tensile
strength of its beauty?

II

If the Floating World, *Ukiyo*, is a nest,

then the rocks and streams
embroidered on the robes of lovers
is not a nest,

> but when they follow the curves
> of their bodies—those curves
> are a nest.

The transient joy of cherry blossoms

is not a nest. But the moment of savoring

       the evanescence of those blossoms
       is a nest. And so it is for lips that make
       wind chimes of words.

A girl viewing plum branches at night,
her lantern held against the negative
space, is not a nest. But negative space,

       the plush black nothingness that holds want—
       that want is a nest.

III
A highway is a bird,
      come, go.

A staircase, a bird,
       ascend, descend.

Yes, the word, a wing.

Reluctant, he pushed her out
of the nest.

Playful, he jostled her into
the nest.

Who's to say what works?

Ruin wants to be a nest. The way it asks,
Are you in?

A crumpled brown bag
is not a nest, though it resembles
a nest, and, once,
could have been one.

Creation of Birds
—after the painting by Remedios Varo

At her drawing table beneath
an open window, the artist
uses her magnifying glass

to refract light from the moon
she nurtures when it's pale.
In her studio, spare as sanctuary,

she grinds nebula, particles
of Saturn, and bits of star cluster—
elixirs to restore it from

its waning presence. In return
it shines a spectral through
the ocular she holds over

her drawings of birds
until they fill with color
and take flight from the page.

I cannot imagine what sound
a painting would make though
I'm certain her heart, a violin,

the strings attached to her pen,
gives her birds song and
the sound of flutter. Part human,

part owl she cannot fly—
the way fish in the deep
sacrifice sight for more

useful senses—the way
her wings have turned
to hands for her birds.

Magritte's Mother's Nightgown

Magritte found his mother's body, nude,
washed up on shore. She threw herself
off a bridge like a bird throwing itself

at the sky. Her nightgown draped over her head,
an image that would appear in his paintings—
phrase repeating, repeating . . . swathed heads,

shrouded heads, mummies who'd come alive
in *Lovers*—a veiled couple drawn to each other,
their eyes adjusted to the gauzy dark.

He painted a bowler-hatted man, his back
to the sea, face obscured by a hovering
green apple. Said we always want to see

what is hidden by what we see. He painted
an apple that filled the entire room,
called it Eve—smooth as the skin of a river—

and surreal as the balloonist who landed
on his childhood home shrouding it
in fabric—his father pulling it through

the window until it filled the room. He painted
an arm reaching for a bird. He painted a bird
made of sky. And a man with the torso

of an empty birdcage. He wore a suit and tie
to paint in his kitchen—his wife, posing,
always nude. She understood pentimento—

the image hidden beneath the surface,
and how a cloth thrown over a cage,
will calm the bird, make it quiet.

A Day at the Lake with Gertrude Stein

It's a morning of sailboats,
    a morning of Gertrude Stein,
and I'm reading her words,
    lounging with her sentences.
It's August, not hot,
    even cool on the point,
the point where dozens of sailboats
    glide easy.
Sky colors the lake,
    precious blue, blue
sails, billowing petals.
    Boats bouquet
drift apart
    while I sit here alone,
alone with Gertrude Stein.
    Leaves flutter green,
green branch swaggers
    swaggers like Picasso's brush—
clouds part to blue,
    roses can't compete,
no rose can compete,
    even a rose can't compete with this.

Defitato

My husband dreams I've won an award
for inventing a word I defined as: "absolutely,
the epitome of being positive." Fitting

since he knows my favorite word is "Yes."
He says we arrive in a limo, I'm wearing
a black sequined dress and he, a tuxedo.

We both look *defitatably* cool. Later, I dream
he's won an award for revising the Fowler
phrenology head—citing a new part of the brain

he calls "the epicurean center" (area of epic cures).
Makes sense since he's a chef who loves science.
At the podium he theorizes: what if everything

we eat turns nutritious in our bodies, inciting
a reaction that would cause our metabolism
to reset itself so that we'd always be

at our ideal weight. Our waiter would ask
if we'd like seconds because eating makes us
epicurious. We'd say, *defitato* Arthur, or Bobo,

and while you're at it, another *obsequikoi*,
my good man (word for the ornamental carp
that resemble flowers swimming). But this genus

is servile, uses flattery as a means of protection
from predators. Example: A barracuda
approaches and the koi says,

Wow, you're looking fabulous!
Your scales shimmer, and your eyes
are not a bit cloudy.

You really think so? says the predator.
Oh, de-fi-tato, Cuda, Koi says. *You smell good too.*
And what if in this epicurean center,

these koi protect our immune system
from turning against itself, and why not
reboot our brains to erase past sorrows,

create a true state of defitato
where dreamers are always welcome
in each others' dream.

Fish Feel Pain

I. ALLERGY: REVENGE OF THE LOBSTER

I'm trying to remember
lobster, its sweet meat,
since I can no longer

consume it. It turned
on me near the shores
of Cape Cod, crept
under my skin—

phantom claws
and spanking tail,
pushing up hives
of spume and spindrift,

the itchy red stigmata—
for all those times
I slipped them
into the boiling pot,
told they really couldn't feel it.

II. TROUT TRAUMA

Today I read that scientists
discovered fish feel pain.

Injecting the lips of trout
with bee venom, they watched them
rock, rub their lips against gravel
for relief. Years ago, fishing

on a cool, clear lake
in the Colorado mountains,
I hooked an 8-pounder;

landed it on the bank, watched
as it flopped and lurched
toward water—

I grabbed a branch to club it,
keep it from getting away
from the dinner table,
thought without a nervous system
it wouldn't feel anything.

III. HUMAN TRAUMA

I've been to the E.R. a few times
with ichthyophagous reactions.
A fillet of haddock turned
my body snapper red,
left me gasping like a fugu
victim at a sushi bar,

and wondering if fish *do* feel
the pain of a baited hook,
walleye, bluegill, and pike flailing
on *Michigan Great Outdoors*,

hanging from the hook of
a finger above the blue-gray pulse
of Lake Erie. And me, gasping,
the release of histamine—
the smother of thin, thin air.

When Chefs Have Nightmares

Not the usual soufflé falling or someone
clouding the consommé he'd been clarifying
for hours—no, this time my husband, Lou,
dreams of a grotesque giant— fungi growing
on a bulbous nose, bloodshot eyes, and
Goliath strong. He breaks into our house and
demands Lou prepare him a warm glass
of milk, says he's taking over his kitchen.

Lou, a graduate of The Culinary Institute,
starts to reach for his Jaccard chrome-plated
meat mallet with interchangeable discs, .
each specifically designed for maximum effect
on various cuts, but the monster grabs him,
paralyzing his arm—his stirring arm,
and forces him to return to the stove.

Lou wakes up, mumbling, terrified, but
says he must return to the dream and wills
himself to fall back asleep. He reaches
into the drawer for a Laguiole steak knife,
razor sharp, with a distinctive steel bee—
symbol of Napoleon's imperial seal. One
awarded to the town of Laguiole for courage
during battle. The monster grabs it

from Lou, attempting to stab him like
an hors d'oeuvre on a toothpick,
prodding him with the tip, toward
the stove to finish warming the milk.

Lou resists again, this time grabbing
a large Santoku knife with a granton edge—
the one used to chop cabbage, parsley,
and slice tomatoes cleanly without crushing
them. He uses it to chop the monster's hand

which resembles the thick, warty rind
of fingered citron, fruit that symbolizes long
life. The monster charges toward him again,
but Lou, like an Iron Chef carving a fresh-
caught squid for calamari al Forno,
finishes him off, returns to his kitchen
to warm the milk— and drink it himself.

Ingratiating the Monster

It may be hard to earn his trust, but
I've seen worse. Men flaunting perfect
abs and smooth complexions yet hideously
empty inside. Become his Franken-Freud.
Analyze his Faustian childhood: controlling
father, hand-me-down body parts, soul-
wrenching rejection.

              "Dear Frankie, big, beautiful-
hearted Frankie, I know, I know Darling,"
you say stroking his chartreuse skin, careful
not to snag your sweater on his hardware:
thick metal bolts, umbilicus that gave him life

through a pair of rusty jumper cables. Ignore
his scent—the scent of tires skidding on tar.
And know that he's self-conscious about his gait,
legs that move like trees uprooting and rerooting.
Remember not to stare at his griddle-flat head,
or the quilt of scars that stitch his blank

yet poignant expression. At night when the clouds
have turned to suede, bring your soft touch to his
bedside, read to him—*Beauty and the Beast*
or *Prometheus*. Pull his patchwork head to your bosom,
and should you notice a murderous rage in his bloodshot
eyes, a quiver in his thin black lips, know that for some,
love can be hard to bear on top of all that wanting.

What Would Hitchcock Do?

I have been notorious for pleading with my husband,
Put the caramels and cupcakes away! Don't let me
fill this old void with ersatz love. We leave the house,
head North by Northwest to an idyllic vacation spot—away

from haunting temptation. He rips off the rear window mirror
cautioning *Don't look back.* Instead we travel to a cottage on a bluff
overlooking a gemmy cobalt sea. A woman with the dreamy eyes
of Kim Novak slipping in and out of her dead great-grandmother's

persona invites us in. She has a birdcage. We don't consider it
a harbinger. But there's a white clapboard bell tower in her yard
that resembles a tall wedding cake. I look up and my head swims,
like the hot fudge on a Sander's cream puff sundae. Reminds me

of the vertigo of childhood when my father, as if spellbound,
became a victim of jealousy around my pretty mother,
forced to leave like some stranger on a train. With his absence,
the emptiness became a neon sign on a cheap motel flashing

VACANCY, VACANCY—a door left open for cravings.
At sunset the bell tower looks dark as chocolate ganache. I try
to imagine the cedar shake roof as something reptilian—alligator
skin, but inevitably it morphs into sugared almonds and praline.

The woman, as if to sabotage what little willpower I have, says
she enjoys drinking espresso with a slice of tiramisu on the porch,
pointing to the parapet. She urges us to follow her up the winding
staircase, which I see as the perfect swirl on a red velvet cupcake.

I hesitate but she reaches out, says, *Are you coming?* Her eyes
have the innocence of a creamy blue sky before a dizzying flock
of birds congregate to destroy an entire town. I remember a line
from a poem: *There are impulses in nature that can't be trusted.*

I cannot be trusted to climb to the summit of a tower that,

come to think of it, reminds me of one of those Harry & David
stacks filled with truffles and petit fours. But then I ask myself,
is all of this merely heavy allegory about a heroine caught

in a psychological struggle over the nature of obsession—
or just a control issue? The woman offers us dessert and like
some psycho, I lose it—grab a knife from her hands, plunging it
into the cake, again and again and again.

Missing Ingredients

I. CABLE GIRL

Surfing through the channels I stop to watch a girl with badly dyed yellow hair pulled into a ponytail, blackened eyebrows, teeth uneven, and her tongue studded in silver. She's sitting on a bed in her own bedroom showing viewers her "wacky finds" for the day. I'm more interested in her quirky imperfections, how she speaks with a pronounced lisp, and how she's packaged what may have been unattractive features into something oddly fascinating. Today there are back-to-back episodes of her show, and my husband, overhearing her, joins me. We follow the host to a tiny kitchen where she holds up a box of Duncan Hines Pineapple Cake Mix. She claims to know nothing at all about baking but thinks it would be fun to make. Searching through her spare cupboards she finds most of the ingredients, is missing the oil, and decides rather than mess up several dishes, "I'll just mix it in the pan," adding an extra egg to make up for the oil. Studying the box again she notices the actual pineapple on top of the cake, removes the soggy rings from a can and lays them over the batter, and then proceeds to bake it, or broil it, at some unknown temperature but one that will severely burn the surface and give the cake an appearance of having attacked itself. When the cake comes out of the oven it matches her dark eyebrows and yellow hair, but she is not dissuaded as she peels away the charred surface, proudly holding the cake alongside the box to show the "amazing similarity." Upon slicing it, the undercooked center oozes a little before it reaches her mouth, as she gushes with a Martha Stewart *"yummm."* My husband's brow freezes, resembling the Gateway Arch when I sigh, "Wish I could be like that."

2. COVER GIRL

My mother blazed her own trail, called the shots. Working to support our family in the late fifties after my father was gone, she saved to buy a modest home in Detroit, and later homes in the suburbs. Mom possessed a wind-in-your-face air, a red-convertible glamour she earned at a job formerly reserved for men. I remember standing in front of her closet, imagining myself going to work in the polka dot dress with matching coat. I marveled at her neat rows of stilettos and pumps, jewelry boxes of pop beads and pearls, and the way she applied her makeup—back when rouge was an art. Each morning she created a flawless image that seemed "perfect," a word she used to describe how things should be done. Yet smart as she was, there were moments she fell into a quirky Stepford trap. A place where the lipstick line smudged in the sand. It made me wonder, what's a cover girl covering up? Her yellow cake with peanut butter frosting was the best thing I ever tasted, but each time she prepared any of her delicious dishes she'd tell us what was missing, how it could have been better, ignoring the praise— as if cake perfection was unattainable. I was confused by these Betty Crocker wanna-be moments. Betty was real to millions. The ultimate cover girl whose picture on the box was a combination of women of all ages and backgrounds so that everyone could become her. My self-image grew to include my father who was interested in how things worked more than how they were packaged. But even now, when Mom says, "Why don't you put on a little red lipstick?"—I struggle, trying not to feel like a cake that can't rise.

Grape Leaves

My grandmother, Sittu, took me for walks down the alley
behind our home in Detroit. There flanking the gravel paths

were old fences that became trellises to grape vines.
She taught me to look for young, tender leaves,

pick them with a delicate touch. Here we'd cross
the divide between us, the clash of cultures

and what it means to be a woman. Her girlhood plucked
early, marriage arranged, femininity was a hard green

grape yanked from the vine. I'd pinch the leaves
using the tips of my fingernails, careful not to yank

or tear as we stacked them midrib to midrib. For her,
so much depended on the meal, the carnal affection

of the dinner table, an intimacy she could enjoy
without shame. Translated from Lebanese, *waraq areesh*

means paper of the vines—unschooled, this was a paper
she could read, the way she read the dandelions she'd pick

for salad mixed with *kishk*,* or tall grasses she'd dye
with red onion peel, weave into baskets. I helped her

blanch the grape leaves to make them pliable, smoothing
the shiny side down, spooning ground lamb, rice, and spices

into the center. She taught me to fold the sides over,
tucking them in as she rolled them into wine cork shapes,

---

* A mixture of cracked wheat soaked in yogurt and dried in the sun.

watched me do the same. We nestled them in the pot
on a rack of lamb riblets, let everything simmer together,

the warmth of those moments, food, our common language
as we reached across fences where the most tender leaves

seemed to say, *pick me, pick me.*

The Meaning of Life

In the Clorox commercial
there's a stream
of washing machines,
one after another
morphing from practical
white to candy apple red,
folks doing laundry
in a continuum from 1913,
long before I was here, back
when Clorox came in amber
bottles, before the white plastic
jug, before trash became
ecological and green.
Aproned mothers—later
men and women less defined,
all part of this strange
but comforting continuity.
And the washing machines,
from wringers to dials
to touch pads but all with
the same purpose—get the dirt
out. It makes me feel a part
of the great pajama drawstring,
a long thread that I've held,
and after I'm gone,
will have been a part of.
It comforts me to know
that Clorox bleaches
out stains, even the ones
left behind.

How to Fall Gently from the Precarious Pedestal

Like the ancient Chinese art of *chi gong*
used to heal our bodies' energies,

or the golden breathing methods of Dr. Lu,
who teaches us how to inhale six

pints of oxygen to feed our vital organs,
so must the keeper of pedestals

teach us the gentle art of falling
off the summit

where some have become addicted
to the rarified air of snow-capped moutaintops.

To descend gracefully, one must honor
the pedestal's transcendental gift,

then look beyond it:
Sit in a comfortable position on your bed.

Relax, like a tired swan. Tilt your head to the heavens.
Let your ears become a black turtle

and listen to the snake behind you.
Now, grab the handle of the big dipper, bringing it down

to your bed. Recline, so your head
rests in the ladle of it. See yourself on a cloud,

sleeping until a red sun rises before you.
Swallow the red sun.

Imagine it falling—gently
changing to a bird, then a fish.

Let it swim with your heart.
Listen to the snow melt.

The Botanist and Her Amaryllis

For twenty years it's the thing
she has lived with the longest,
nurtured from a bulb.
She cultivated an appreciation
for tropical ornamentation,
the funneled startle
of red, the green gesture
of photosynthesis.
She sees the verdant aura
of chlorophyll,
its microcrystalline pigment,
senses the conversion of light
into chemical energy,
knows the deep secrets
of roots—her voice
like anthers
whispering pollen.

To Be Fed

To prepare a feast, Uke Mochi, Shinto goddess of food,
        faced the sea and spit out a fish. At the forest's edge
game flew from her orifices. Eyeing a rice paddy she
        coughed up bowls of rice. When Tsukiyomi, moon god
she wanted to please, killed her in disgust, her corpse

turned to millet and beans. In *Babette's Feast*, Babette was no
        goddess but a woman worshipped. When her family is murdered
she retreats, becomes a servant to strict Lutheran sisters,
        preparing simple food but better than the bread-ale soup
they'd been eating every day. Later she wins the lottery using

the entire sum to prepare a meal uniting spirit and flesh:
        caviar, terrapin soup, quail with truffled foie gras, fine
wines, and sumptuous pastries. I think of heartbroken Tita from
        Like Water for Chocolate, forced to cook
the wedding dinner for her sister's marriage to Pedro,

the man she herself loves. She pricks her finger on a thorn
        while preparing quail with sauce made of rose petals
Pedro had given her. The dish, fragrant and sensual, embodies
        her lust and sadness, leaving the guests to weep as they dine.
I watched my grandmother transform flour

into savory pies and sweet pastries, followed the curled
        finger of aroma inviting me in. Later, I'd summon
my inner Aphrodite to make heart-shaped cakes
        on Valentine's Day. Send warm banana nut bread
to seduce the boy across the street, his father assuring me

he'd deliver it, later asking for more, saying
        he thinks it's working. Before the Shinto goddess slept,
she poured herself into the river where the moon god
        kept his reflection. I wonder if he tasted
her sweetness when that river turned to honey?

Baklava Killed My Father

It was the Lebanese pastry my father loved,
different from the Greek. Pistachios
more than walnuts, syrup not honey.

Preheat oven to 350°.

He had an appetite for layers, learned French,
English, and Arabic in school, later Italian,
Portuguese, Spanish, German, and Greek.

Butter a 10-by-14-inch baking pan.

Lebanese fables are similar to Greek myths,
Tantalus sentenced to stand eternally in a pool of water
that recedes when he tries to drink, and under
a tree, ripe fruit just out of his reach.

For the filling, combine 3 cups chopped pistachios,
⅓ cup sugar, and 1 tablespoon rosewater in bowl.
Set aside.

The way Scheherazade, in *A Thousand and One*
Arabian Nights, tantalized the king to save herself,
reciting only the beginning of a new tale every
evening. The king forced to spare her— eager to hear
the end of her never-ending story.

Unwrap and carefully unfold 1 pound thawed phyllo dough.

My father dined in beautiful settings around the world,
red snapper in Algiers, ratatouille in Provence,
octopus near the Athens Acropolis.

Cover with a wet cloth, as it will dry out quickly.

When I saw him, after an eight-year absence, his belly
had grown round as a globe,

Begin to layer half of the dough in prepared pan.

the image of Bacchus, drinking and feasting,
his fennel staff wound with ivy, dripping with honey.

Using 1¼ cups clarified butter, coat each layer
with a pastry brush.

Dad sent postcards and letters, always in his signature
green ink, a color that meant father but also meant gone.

Halfway through the layering, spread pistachio
mixture to an even thickness.

He sent a photo, posing next to David's
Death of Socrates, philosopher who said
"The only true wisdom is in knowing
you know nothing."

Continue layering buttered phyllo.

Father searched the world for someone
he could relate to, realizing too late, he said,
it was the daughter he had left behind.

Bring 2 cups sugar and 1 cup water to a boil for syrup.
Boil 2 minutes. Add 1 tablespoon fresh lemon juice
and 1 tablespoon rosewater; boil 10 seconds more.

The Greeks feasted on ambrosia and honey,
fragrant confections, an offering to appease the gods.

Cut the baklava into diamond-shaped pieces
pouring the cooled syrup over the hot pastry
until it is well saturated.

My father craved, couldn't resist the ethereal
crunch of baklava—dangerous for his diabetes,
but deliciously sweet, and rosewater scented.

Music from Another Room

There was a time when family and friends gathered around
our mahogany table to dine on creamy hummus—baba ganoush
sprinkled with paprika, drizzled with olive oil. I can taste the vibrant
green of the tabouli, the tart contrast of sumac on toasty fattoush
salad, sweet tomatoes, bright tang of lemons, and the grassy scent
released from hand-chopped parsley. I still picture tender rice glistening
with thin vermicelli surrounded by cinnamon bronzed roast chicken. And
my father serving platters of grilled kabobs, the caramelized aroma
of charred onions, buttery hints of pine-nut and minced lamb layered
into baked kibbe scored into diamonds—raw kibbe, a tartare with hints
of green pepper and orange zest. Sittu's plump stuffed grape leaves,
Mom's green beans coated in garlicky tomato—and baskets of soft pita
to scoop it all up. Everything fresh from the farmer stalls of Detroit's
Eastern Market where Dad shopped at dawn balancing armfuls of bags.

Home is where I learned the music of the kitchen: the rhythmic cutting,
chopping, dicing, cymbal gongs of pots and pans landing on iron grates,
fanning cupboards, snapping drawers, the clink of silver on china
when cardamom-scented Turkish coffee was poured. Here I found art
in the jeweled still life of pomegranates, grapes, figs, and apricots—bowls
of pistachios, pastel candied chickpeas— fragrant rosewater wafting from
silver trays stacked with crisp baklava and date-filled *ma'amoul* cookies.
Everyone dressed for dinner—neck-tied men, skirted women jangling gold
bangles as they passed savory platters. How I miss the tenor of voices rising
and falling, ripple and trill of bilingual tongues, the shuffle of decks, crash
of poker chips during all-night card games, the dancing—our living room
alive with cadenced clapping, hips swiveling to the ouds and derbekes
of Port Said, the hand-held chain of the dabke line dance, and soulful
ballads of Fairuz. Later, all eyes on Sittu who read our fortunes in coffee
grounds clinging to the porcelain cups—a letter arriving, a trip to be taken,
a relative coming from a distant land—a distant time, elusive now—I can't
remember the chairs ever being empty—the table bare and quiet as dust.

Strings Attached

Mother was an Edward Hopper painting—a woman drawn
to a wedge of sunlight, an oil drum rolling down a quiet
street at night. At thirteen she sailed from New York

to Lebanon—wouldn't take her eyes off the Statue of Liberty.
She was the house by the railroad, an airmail envelope arriving,
departing—the new girl who refused to sing the Lebanese anthem.

Her marriage arranged at fifteen, she rode off on a white horse
with a good Druze man. He couldn't take his eyes off her.
She walked barefoot on hot gravel from Beirut to Bekefa

to persuade my father to move to New York, and they did.
Mother was beautiful as Sophia Loren—a perfumed scarf grazing
as she floated by—the red curtain rising in a movie theater.

Divorced at twenty-three, *Woman's Day* called her "A pint-size
gal in a man-size job." She wore chemise dresses and high-heels,
drove company cars, won trips to Europe. I called her

Miro's ladder receding into the night sky—the moon
and the bird who couldn't hear the dog barking down below.
Mom was fluent in Arabic but never spoke it, changed

her name from Fadwa to Freda— baked shepherd pies
and Johnny cakes, cooked *fasoulia* for company. She believed
in freedom, let us choose our own religion. We worshipped her.

My mother loved Tchaikovsky's concertos, Rubáiyát poetry,
and poker till dawn. She was modern art, a light
in the window—never the apron, or even the strings.